For

_____,

who officially graduated from

_____

institution

on

_____

date

Congratulations from

_____

OUR PURPOSE AT HOWARD PUBLISHING IS TO:

- *Increase faith* in the hearts of growing Christians
- *Inspire holiness* in the lives of believers
- *Instill hope* in the hearts of struggling people everywhere

BECAUSE HE'S COMING AGAIN!

Published by Howard Publishing Co., Inc.
3117 North 7th Street, West Monroe, Louisiana 71291-2227

03 04 05 06 07 08 09 10 11 12   10 9 8 7 6 5 4 3 2 1

Edited by Between the Lines
Interior design by Stephanie Denney
Illustrations by Kristy Caldwell
Cover design by LinDee Loveland

Library of Congress Cataloging-in-Publication Data
  Bolton, Martha, 1951–
    The "official" grad book : the who, what, when, where, why, and how of being a grad
  Martha Bolton ; illustrated by Kristy Caldwell.
      p. cm.
    ISBN: 1-58229-300-7; ISBN: 1-58229-305-8 (softcover)
      1. High schools—United States—Miscellanea. 2. Universitites and colleges—United States—Miscellanea. 3. Conduct of life—Miscellanea. 4. Gift books. I. Title.

LB1602 .B65 2002
371.2'912—dc21

2002191258

THE "official"

grad BOOK

The Who, What,
When, Where,
Why, and How
of Being a **Grad**
Illustrated by Kristy Caldwell

HOWARD
PUBLISHING CO.

**Martha
Bolton**

Contents

◆

You did it!

**The roots of true achievement lie in the will
to become the best that you can become.**

Harold Taylor

You Did It!

You did it! It wasn't easy, but you did it! The homework, the pop quizzes, the term papers, the finals—everything that has made your life miserable for the past twelve, fourteen, sixteen, or however many years it has taken—is now over. It's time to celebrate!

Nothing that's worthwhile in life comes easily. But you stayed on task, and you've earned something that a lot of people never get to have—a diploma. It's yours. No matter what else you accomplish in life, or don't accomplish, this one is yours to keep. You can't lose it in the stock market. You can't transfer it to the highest bidder on eBay. You can't even pass it down to your children or grandchildren. This is your diploma—yours alone, and yours forever. Enjoy!

THE who OF BEING A GRAD

*A graduate is someone who has eaten
every item in the school cafeteria and lived to tell about it.*

> **I think sleeping was my problem in school.**
> **If school had started at four o'clock in the afternoon,**
> **I'd be a college graduate today.**
>
> ◆
>
> George Foreman

Who Is a Graduate?

According to the dictionary, the definition of a graduate is, "A person who has received a degree or diploma on completing a course of study, as in a university, college, or school."

But there's a lot more to it than that.

A graduate is SOMEONE WHO
has eaten every item in the school cafeteria (the good, the bad, and the ugly) and lived to tell about it.

A graduate is SOMEONE WHO

has been cleaning out his locker for the last three months and donating a year's supply of new cultures to the chemistry lab.

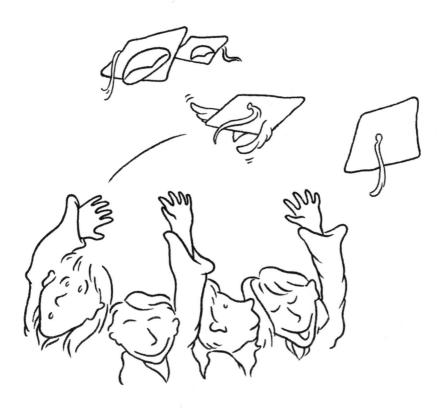

A graduate is SOMEONE WHO
can toss her cap in the air with
twelve hundred other caps and still believe
she'll be able to find her own again.

A graduate is SOMEONE WHO
diets all year to look good in a graduation gown
two sizes too large.

A graduate is SOMEONE WHO
gets to resell four hundred dollars'
worth of college textbooks for twenty-six bucks.

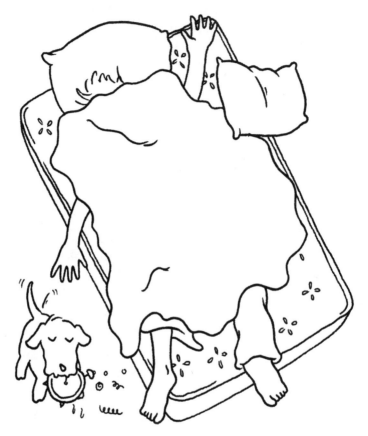

A graduate is SOMEONE WHO
can finally sleep in and not need an excuse.

A graduate is SOMEONE WHO
can look forward to a future full of new possibilities,
new adventures, new friends, and old student-loan payments!

You know who you are.

**God can make you anything you want to be,
but you have to put everything in His hands.**

Mahalia Jackson

Nametags

Have you ever hesitated when someone asked your name? Have you ever walked around at a party, reunion, or other gathering wearing a blank nametag? When filling out a job or other application, have you ever had to pause at the line that says "Name"?

My name? Oh, great…it's the first line of the application, and already they're asking the hard questions!

We all know our names. We can write them on nametags and quickly answer whenever someone asks us to identify ourselves. When filling out an application, we don't have to call our parents to ask what we should write on that line that says "Name." We know what to write. We know who we are.

After graduation, though, in the rush for success, we can forget who we are—at least who we are inside. New friends replace old ones, new values replace old values, and new ambitions replace former dreams.

As you pursue success in life, don't forget to take the real you along too. Don't sell out. Don't build your career while destroying your foundation. Taking new paths in life is fine, but don't forget the journey you've already taken. Be true to yourself. The name on the nametag hasn't changed.

In the rush for success,
we can forget who we are.

What we are is God's gift to us.

What we become is our gift to God.

Eleanor Powell

A graduation ceremony is an event

where the commencement speaker tells

thousands of students dressed in identical caps and gowns

that "individuality" is the key to success.

Robert Orben

**It takes courage to grow up
and become who you really are.**

E. E. Cummings

There's Only One You

The most important thing for comedians to remember is to be themselves. That's where the best comedy is going to come from. Jay Leno can't tell jokes about Bill Cosby's life. Only Bill can. Jerry Seinfeld can't tell jokes about Ray Romano's life. Only Ray can.

The world has enough duplicates. It needs originals. If you're focusing all your efforts on trying to be exactly like someone else, you're wasting your life and the world's time. We don't want to see someone who can act just like Dustin Hoffman. We have Dustin Hoffman. Why do we need a copy? We don't want to see someone who can sing like Celine Dion. We have Celine Dion. We already know what she can do. We need to see what you can do.

So be yourself. You're the one who will do the best job of being you.

The World Didn't Know

what Beethoven had to offer until he played it.

The World Didn't Know

what Shakespeare had to offer until he wrote it.

The World Didn't Know

what Einstein had to offer until

he calculated it.

The World Didn't Know

what Thomas Edison had to offer

until he invented it.

The World Didn't Know

what Michelangelo had to offer

until he painted it.

The World Doesn't Know

what you have to offer until you give it.

The world is waiting.

When I stand before God

at the end of my life,

I would hope that I would not

have a single bit of talent left

and could say,

"I used everything You gave me."

Erma Bombeck

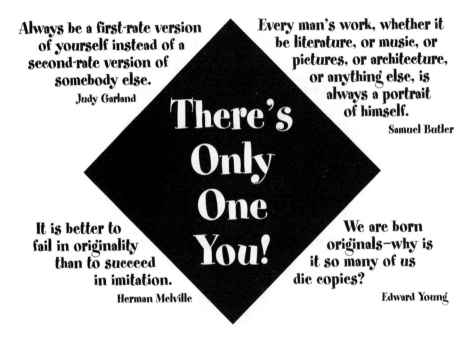

Always be a first-rate version of yourself instead of a second-rate version of somebody else.
Judy Garland

Every man's work, whether it be literature, or music, or pictures, or architecture, or anything else, is always a portrait of himself.
Samuel Butler

There's Only One You!

It is better to fail in originality than to succeed in imitation.
Herman Melville

We are born originals—why is it so many of us die copies?
Edward Young

Going against the Flow

I have a magnet on my refrigerator that says, "Trust your crazy ideas." It's next to one that says, "Warning: Leftovers may be hazardous to your health." They're both good advice. But "Trust your crazy ideas" is something that will help you throughout your entire life, not just at mealtime.

To achieve great things, sometimes you have to trust your crazy ideas.

Sometimes to achieve great things, you have to go against the flow. You have to stick your neck out. You have to trust your crazy ideas. I'm sure people laughed when the Wright brothers told them they were building a machine that would enable man to fly: "I don't care what you're working on—we came to the beach to have fun. Now put that contraption away, and let's go surfing!"

Or when Henry Ford said he wanted to spend every spare moment working on an invention to mass-produce automobiles that would one day take people from place to place and clog every freeway in the world during rush hour.

And don't forget Alexander Graham Bell, Thomas Edison, and George Washington Carver. They all had crazy ideas—ideas that turned out to be pure genius.

Everyone who has ever achieved greatness has had to take certain risks. Just about everything in life involves some risk. When you fall in love, you're taking a risk that your heart will get broken. Eating food can be a risk: You could swallow something the wrong way and choke.

Just breathing is a risk: Who knows if you'll catch a virus, inhale bacteria, or have morning breath that could kill?

Even though breathing is risky, you don't see all that many people walking around sporting gas masks, do you? That's because we've learned to cope with those risks. And we can learn to cope with the risks of achieving our goals. Don't get me wrong, we should certainly be wise when it comes to our safety; but when it comes to the pursuit of our dreams, we need to be focused, brave, and committed.

Henry Ford, the Wright brothers, Thomas Edison, and a host of others stayed focused on their "crazy ideas" and achieved great things. They had plenty of failures along the way, but they didn't let those failures deter them from their mission. They remained committed and eventually saw the fruits of their labor.

And who was laughing then?

**If they give you ruled paper,
write the other way.**

Juan Ramon Jimenez

A man who trims himself

to suit everybody will

soon whittle himself away.

Charles Schwab

> **Great artists are people who find the way to be themselves in their art.**

Margot Fonteyn

Historical Yearbooks

Yearbooks have always been a great place to pen that parting sentiment to friends, to let them know how much they've meant to you over the last semester or throughout your life. Years later it's fun to read through these yearbooks and be reminded of our schooldays. Some yearbooks probably have even had historical significance.

Or not...

Written in George Washington's yearbook:

George, it's been fun sitting behind you in class this year.
Sorry about the pigtail in the inkwell thing. But you have to admit it was
pretty funny. Have a great summer!

Charlie

Written in Benjamin Franklin's yearbook:

I've never quite known how to tell you this, Ben, but you're an adult now.
Kite flying is, well, you know, kinda childish. You really need to get
a different hobby. Or at least quit doing it in thunderstorms.
You're gonna get yourself killed, bro! I'm only saying this because
we're friends. Anyhoo, best of luck in everything you do in life!
Buford

Written in Alexander Graham Bell's yearbook:

Call me.
Sarah

Written in Jonah's yearbook:

Hey! Heard you were going to Tarshish. Is that true?
I always figured you'd end up in Nineveh. Don't know why.
Just a feeling, I guess. Oh well, happy sailing.
Hang ten, dude!
Matt

Written in Socrates' yearbook:

Thanks for all the advice you've given me this past semester, Soc.

You're really a smart guy. Maybe you'll be a philosopher or something.

Or work in fast food with me. Hey, maybe they could put your sayings

on the french-fry bags. Cool, huh?

Curtis

Written in Michelangelo's yearbook:

Hi, Mikey! Loved sitting next to you in art class!

Hope lots of great things are in store for you.

But you gotta quit painting on walls and ceilings, man.

I don't think that's legal.

Dominique

Who Can Stop You?

Who can focus on the obstacles and not on
the destination?

Who can listen to discouragers instead of
encouragers?

Who can count the cost and not the gain?

Who can convince you that it's too hard?

Who can give up on your dreams?

Who can give in to insecurities?

Who can feel overwhelmed?

Who can feel undeserving?

Who can procrastinate?

Who can stop working?

Who can feel inferior?

Who can quit trying?

Only one person

can stop you—

YOU.

**A great deal of talent is lost to the world
for want of a little courage.**

Sydney Smith

Silent gratitude isn't much use to anyone.

G. B. Stern

To Whom Credit Is Due

Accomplishments are seldom achieved in a vacuum. As you walk across the platform to receive your diploma, your thoughts go to the person or persons who helped you get to this remarkable place in your life. Teachers, parents, friends, grandparents, your principal, your pastor, your youth pastor, neighbors, aunts, uncles—some or all of these people have played a role in your education and achievements.

Maybe they packed your lunch every day since kindergarten; maybe they helped you with your homework or drove you to and from school for all those extracurricular activities. Perhaps they helped you sound out words in first grade or went over your lines with you for your tenth-grade drama class. It could be that they gave you advice on your sixth-grade science project or on which college to attend. Or maybe they were just there to lend a listening ear whenever you needed it.

Whatever they did to help you, encourage you, and support you, this is the perfect time to say thanks. Give credit where credit is due. Do it today.

There are high spots in all of our lives, and most of them have come about through encouragement from someone else. I don't care how great, how famous, or successful a man or woman may be, each hungers for applause.

George Matthew Adams

Teachers

Teachers—you've had your good ones and you've had your...well, maybe you've had one or two who didn't leave you with many fond memories. But whether they were understanding or difficult, kind or unbelievably strict, you learned something from each of them. And whatever they did, they must have done something right, because you've arrived at this point in your life. You've earned your diploma. You're not receiving it because they needed your seat for an incoming student. They're not giving it to you out of pity because you're the only senior with gray hair. You're receiving your diploma because you earned it. You listened in class, studied your books, completed your work, and now you've passed. Your teachers have successfully imparted a portion of their knowledge, and hopefully their passion for their subject, into your mind and life. Thank them for it.

The mediocre teacher tells. The good teacher explains. The superior teacher demonstrates. The great teacher inspires.

William Arthur Ward

Family

Parents, grandparents, aunts, uncles—a lot of people have invested time and energy into your life. They're proud of you. This is the day they'll look themselves in the mirror and say, "It was worth it all." Every science fair, every parent-teacher conference, all the homework that was over their heads but they helped you with anyway—this occasion was worth it all. You're a graduate. You've accomplished what they wanted you to accomplish. You've accomplished what you wanted to accomplish. Let your family know how much their support has meant to you.

**Your families are extremely proud of you.
You can't imagine the sense of relief
they are experiencing.
This would be a most opportune time
to ask for money.**

Gary Bolding

Friends

Your friends have helped you get to this place in your life too. Friends and the daily encouragement they provide play a major role in whatever we achieve in life. Certainly we all have superficial friends; but true friends, those who have remained faithful in both the good times and the bad, deserve your thanks.

A faithful friend is a strong defense; and he that hath found him hath found a treasure.

Louisa May Alcott

God

There's been a lot of debate as to whether prayer should be allowed in school. Many graduates admit, however, that they couldn't have made it to this moment in their lives without their personal prayers.

They prayed before every test and every pop quiz. They prayed that the bell wouldn't ring as they were running late to class. They prayed before football games and cheerleader tryouts. They prayed for their relationships when a boyfriend or girlfriend met them in the hallway and told them they wanted to break up. They prayed when bullies teased them. Despite a handful of protestors, there always has been—and always will be—a lot of prayer going on at school.

> *I am the LORD,*
> *your God, who takes*
> *hold of your right hand*
> *and says to you,*
> *Do not fear;*
> *I will help you.*
>
> —Isaiah 41:13

If you're a person of faith, you know that God has been with you each step of the way, from grade to grade, school to school. Graduation is a good time to thank Him for His faithfulness.

Do not be anxious about anything,

but in everything, by prayer and petition, with

thanksgiving, present your requests

to God. And the peace of God,

which transcends all understanding,

will guard your hearts and

your minds in Christ Jesus.

—Philippians 4:6–7

THE what

OF BEING

A GRAD

Is that really a diploma or just a hall pass?

> The world is round, and the place which may seem
> like the end may also be the beginning.

Ivy Baker Priest

The Accomplishment

You did it! You met the requirements, completed your classwork, didn't slack off on your homework, scored high enough on your tests, and now you're being handed the prize—your diploma. Good job!

Friends and family have gathered to watch you graduate. They're proud, excited, and, after all the graduation expenses, probably broke. A few relatives might even have a difficult time hiding their feelings of surprise: *Is that really a diploma or just a hall pass?*

But that's OK. All that matters is, you did it! You've earned your diploma. This is your moment in the spotlight. Shine!

Your moment to shine!

A Diploma Is...
validation
inspiration
praise
encouragement
completion
approval
achievement
forever

What You'll Never Hear on Graduation Night

Look at all the available parking spaces!

I brought way too much film.

Tissue? No thanks. I'm not going to cry.

What You'll Never Hear...

I've got extra tickets to the ceremony.
Anybody need them?

Whad'ya mean there's no homework tonight?

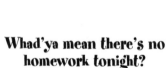

Now, parents, there's to be no cheering.

...on Graduation Night

Hey, Teach, I guess those cheat sheets really worked, huh?

Those speeches were way too short.

I'm glad my last name starts with Z.

The Process

Education is learning what you didn't even know

you didn't even know.

◆

Daniel J. Boorstin

Perhaps the most valuable result of all education is the ability

to make yourself do the thing you have to do

when it ought to be done,

whether you like it or not.

◆

Walter Bagehot

Diligence is the mother of good luck.

◆

Benjamin Franklin

I come to the office each morning and stay for long hours

doing what has to be done to the best of my ability.

And when you've done the best you can,

you can't do any better.

So when I go to sleep

I turn everything over to the Lord and forget it.

◆

Harry S. Truman

Education is what's left over

when you subtract what you've forgotten

from what you've learned.

◆

Lloyd Cory

Blessed is he who submits to the will of God;
he can never be unhappy.

Martin Luther

The Plan

God has a plan FOR YOUR LIFE
—don't underestimate it.

God has a plan FOR YOUR LIFE
—don't doubt it.

God has a plan FOR YOUR LIFE
—don't ignore it.

God has a plan FOR YOUR LIFE
—don't complicate it.

God has a plan FOR YOUR LIFE
—don't give up on it.

God has a plan FOR YOUR LIFE
—don't discount it.

God has a plan FOR YOUR LIFE
—don't fear it.

God has a plan FOR YOUR LIFE
—don't settle for less.

God has a plan FOR YOUR LIFE
—don't go around it.

God has a plan FOR YOUR LIFE
—don't let Him down.

Do not pray for tasks equal to your powers. Pray for power equal to your tasks.
Phillips Brooks

Promotion cometh neither from the east, nor from the west,

nor from the south. But God is the judge:

he putteth down one, and setteth up another.

—Psalm 75:6–7 KJV

...In other words, promotion comes from the north.

Obstacles are those frightful things you see when you take your eyes off your goal.

◆

Henry Ford

God prepares great men
for great tasks by great trials.

J. K. Gressett

The Obstacles

Nothing worthwhile comes easily, least of all success. There's work to be done. There are papers to complete, tests to take, and obstacles to overcome. Ah yes. Obstacles. No doubt you've already encountered a few of those on your path to this moment. Maybe you've encountered more than your share. And even though it is said "The greater the adversity the greater the triumph," most of us would settle for a little less triumph and a lot less adversity. But that's not life. We don't get to choose the size of the obstacles in our path or the magnitude of our victories. If we did, major obstacles would never be overcome, because nobody would ever choose them. Who among us would select a serious illness over a traffic jam, or the loss of a loved one over an overdue utility bill? Nobody. But we don't get to pick which obstacles we will face in life. We have to take them as they come our way. One by one, one day at a time.

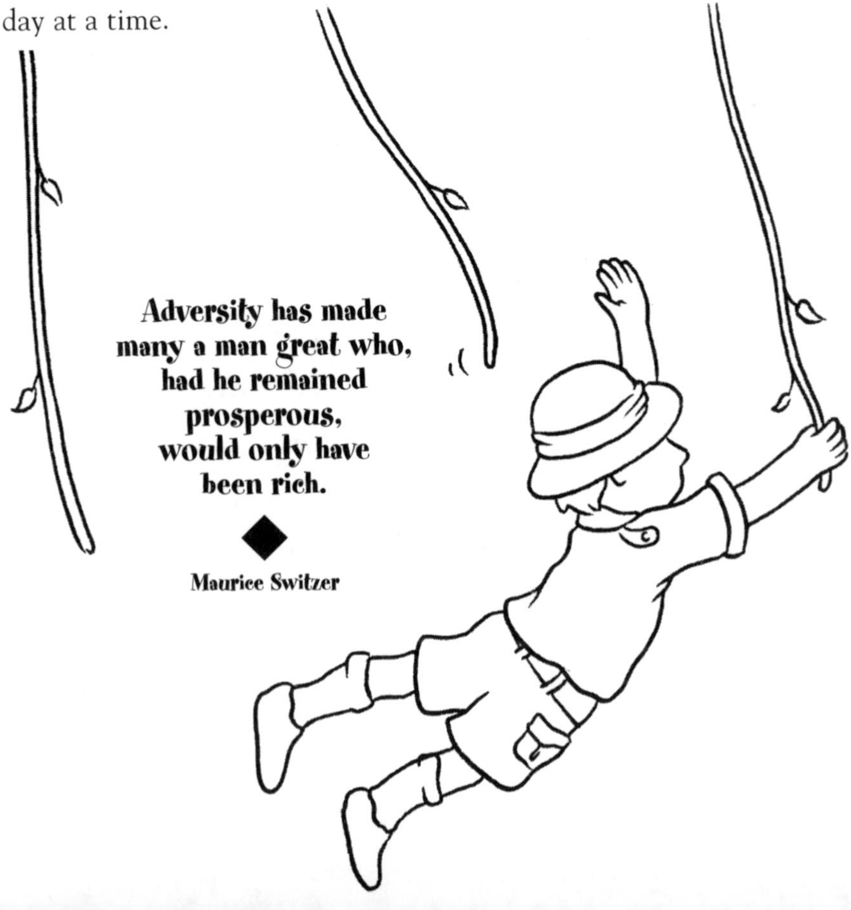

Adversity has made many a man great who, had he remained prosperous, would only have been rich.

◆

Maurice Switzer

What on earth would a man
do with himself
if something did not
stand in his way?

◆

H. G. Wells

The Requirements

Be Available

It seems to me that those songs that have been any good,

I have nothing much to do with the writing of them.

The words have just crawled down my sleeve and come out on the page.

◆

Joan Baez

Be Courageous

Courage is contagious. When a brave man takes a stand,

the spines of others are often stiffened.

◆

Billy Graham

Be Open-Minded

BLAH BLAH BLAH

A fool finds no pleasure
in understanding
but delights in airing his
own opinions.

◆

Proverbs 18:2

Be Trusting

Never be afraid to trust an unknown future to a known God.

◆

Corrie Ten Boom

Be Resilient

I've always grown from my problems and challenges, from the things that don't work out—that's when I've really learned.

◆

Carol Burnett

Be an Original Thinker

What a good thing Adam had. When he said a good thing,

he knew nobody had said it before.

◆

Mark Twain

Be at Peace

You will keep in perfect peace him whose mind is steadfast,

because he trusts in you.

◆

Isaiah 26:3

Graduation means transitioning from one phase of life to another.

Write injuries in dust, benefits in marble.

Benjamin Franklin

The Good-Byes

In all the preparation for the big day, we often don't think about the pain that comes with a graduation. I'm not talking about being given a cap that's too tight. That can happen too, of course. What I'm talking about is the pain of leaving behind friends with whom, no matter how much we promise to stay in touch, we lose touch. Graduation also means transitioning from one phase of life to another, and that can be painful. For some, it means walking across the stage in four-inch heels. That too can be painful. And it means receiving the freedom we thought we so desperately wanted only to discover it feels a lot scarier than we ever expected.

What comes next?

Yes, even though graduation is a time for celebration, it also hurts as we say good-bye to friends, teachers, and at least officially, a part of our youth.

A friendship can weather most things and thrive in thin soil—but it needs a little mulch of letters and phone calls and small, silly presents every so often—just to save it from drying out completely.

Pam Brown

All that stands between the graduate and the top of the ladder is the ladder.

Anonymous

What Comes Next?

Don't be afraid of hard work. Chances are you've already garnered plenty of experience staying up until two o'clock in the morning completing term papers. Maybe you don't think those experiences taught you anything besides how to better gauge your time, but they did. They taught you that when your back is against the wall, you can rise to the occasion and get the work done. You know you can depend on yourself to sacrifice a little sleep to accomplish something. You know you can follow through.

Knowing that you can accomplish a task will give you confidence to accept new assignments that will stretch you. You know that even though the work is difficult, you won't give up until you get it done.

You know you're not a quitter. You know you don't turn in half-finished projects. You know you don't give up. That's an important quality, and it's important to know you have it.

**Opportunities
are usually
disguised as hard work,
so most people don't
recognize them.**

◆

Ann Landers

Never take counsel of your fears.

Andrew Jackson

The Future

So what happens now, after the graduation ceremony? After all the graduation parties? Have you filled in that section in your day planner called "The Rest of Your Life"? Or did you simply write down the letters TBA (to be announced) and buy yourself some more time to think?

It's not always easy to know what to do after graduation. It's finally time for you to start making life choices, and you worry whether you'll make the right ones. Maybe you're already feeling the pressure, with relatives and friends asking what you're going to do for the next sixty or seventy years.

If the future is looking a little scary, relax. As Abraham Lincoln once reminded us, the future only comes one day at a time.

Take a
chance!
All life is a chance.
The man who goes furthest
is generally the one who is
willing to do
and dare.

Dale Carnegie

Always take a job that is too big for you,

and then do your best.

◆

Harry Emerson Fosdick

Nature does not demand that we be perfect.

It requires only that we grow.

◆

Josh Loth Liebman

THE when
OF BEING
A GRAD

Don't spend your todays
regretting the botched
plans of yesterday.
Life's too short to
waste a single day.

Lost, yesterday, somewhere between sunrise and sunset, two golden hours, each set with sixty diamond minutes. No reward is offered, for they are gone forever.

Horace Mann

Yesterday

The past is the past. No matter how much you'd like for it to come back, it won't. Wish you had graduated with a better grade point average? Wish you had caught that pass and scored that touchdown during the homecoming game? Wish you had never changed your major? Sorry, but you can't change any of it. That was yesterday, and it's gone.

Looking back is fine as long as we don't allow it to handicap our present or future. It's good to see the positives of yesterday and learn from the negatives, but to spend our todays regretting the wrong decisions, missed plays, or botched plans of yesterday is to waste our lives. And life's too short to waste a single day of it.

Take care
of the minutes,
for the hours
will take care
of themselves.

Lord Chesterfield

**Let him who would enjoy a good future
waste none of his present.**

Dale Carnegie

Today

We can learn from yesterday, and we can hope for tomorrow; but today is what's tangible. It's the here and now. It's the present. The accomplishments of yesterday are in the past. Tomorrow's dreams are yet to be realized. Today is where the majority of our focus needs to be. Today is what has been entrusted to us. We've been given our lives to live one day at a time. Don't waste what is and what still can be by constantly looking back at what might have been.

The secret of getting ahead is getting started.

Sally Berger

Don't wait
> for acceptance.

Don't wait
> for encouragement.

Don't wait
> for more time.

Don't wait
> for someone to recognize your talents.

Don't wait
> for more confidence.

Don't wait
> for less stress in your life.

Don't wait
> for more money.

Don't wait
> for others to help you.

Don't wait
> for permission to succeed.

Don't wait
> to step into your future.

While we are postponing, life speeds by.

Seneca

A goal is nothing more than a dream with a time limit.

Joe L. Griffith

*I don't think much of a man who
is not wiser today than he was yesterday.*

Abraham Lincoln

Tomorrow isn't where our vacations hide out;
it's the "To Be Continued" of our lives.

Procrastination is the art of keeping up with yesterday.

Matthew Mittleman

Tomorrow

Tomorrow wasn't intended to be a catchall for the projects we didn't get to today. It's not a place to park our dreams and goals, then never get around to them. Tomorrow isn't where our vacations hide out or our riches elude us.

Tomorrow isn't detached from today. It's an extension of it. It's overtime.

It's an allotment of more hours to finish whatever work we started today but couldn't quite finish.

It's the "To Be Continued" of our lives.

It's the sequel.

It's Part II and III and IV and so on.

It's where we continue to pursue our dreams, not bury them.

All of our tomorrows will come to us in single file, one at a time, separated from today by a mere whisper of time. Look forward to your tomorrows, but don't fall into the trap of living in them.

Time Waits for No One

The secret of success in life is for a man to be ready
for his opportunity when it comes.

◆

Benjamin Disraeli

Dream as if you'll live forever. Live as if you'll die today.

◆

James Dean

If the Dream Fits

Do you know instinctively what you're supposed to be doing with your life but find yourself changing your mind time and time again, trying to please those around you? To accomplish what you are destined to accomplish in your lifetime, you have to trust your own instincts. You must have confidence in your own judgment, your own ideas, and your own capabilities. Even if the task seems overwhelming, you can have confidence in your ability to get it done because you know you're doing what you were created to do. Those around you may not know or appreciate this purpose, but you know it; and it's up to you to have the dedication and the single-mindedness to get it done.

There's nothing sadder than an elderly person looking back on his life knowing that he "missed it." Somewhere along the line, he surrendered his dream too easily, and now he's left with a lifetime of regrets.

You're writing the script of your life right now. This is the only script, even with all the edits and rewrites, that you'll have to look back on someday, so write it with everything you have in you. Don't hold anything back. Make it a script you'll be proud of when it's finished.

Don't just stand there. Make it happen.

◆

Lee Iacocca

Laugh at yourself, but don't ever aim your doubt at yourself.
Be bold. When you embark for strange places,
don't leave any of yourself safely on shore.
Have the nerve to go into unexplored territory.

◆

Alan Alda

The people who get on in this world
are the people who get up and look for the circumstances they want and,
if they can't find them, make them.

◆

George Bernard Shaw

Use what talents you possess;
the woods would be very silent if no birds sang
except those that sang best.

◆

Henry Van Dyke

The opportunity that God sends does not wake up him who is asleep.

◆

Senegalese proverb

God gives every bird its food,
but He does not throw it into the nest.

J. G. Holland

 # A Wait Problem

While you're waiting FOR MORE TIME,
you're wasting time.

While you're waiting FOR THE RIGHT DOOR TO OPEN,
you could be walking by
the right door that's already open.

While you're waiting FOR MORE MONEY,
it's costing you money.

While you're waiting FOR ENCOURAGEMENT,
you might not be hearing the encouragement
you're being given right now.

While you're waiting FOR PERMISSION TO SUCCEED,
you are giving yourself permission to fail.

Time As Teacher

Even after graduation, one teacher will remain with you for the rest of your life. That teacher is Time. Time can be a tough educator. You can try your best to persuade Time to turn back and let you relive some

*Time only operates
in a forward direction.*

moments in your past, but it won't do it. It can't. Time can only operate in a forward direction. We turn our clocks back one hour every autumn, but we're not stopping time. Time marches on in spite of anything we do to try to stop or delay it.

The lessons Time teaches are valuable ones. And unlike all those historical dates you studied for a test but forgot soon afterward, lessons learned through Time have a way of working themselves into your brain and staying there for good. Some of the lessons will be fun. Some will be painful. But the more we can learn from Time, the easier our future will be.

*Some lessons
are painful.*

The trouble with learning from experience

is that you never graduate.

◆

Doug Larson

No day in which you learn

something is a complete loss.

◆

David Eddings

Graduation is only a concept.

In real life every day you graduate.

Graduation is a process that goes on

until the last day of your life.

If you can grasp that,

you'll make a difference.

◆

Arie Pencovici

**Don't be afraid your life will end;
be afraid that it will never begin.**

Grace Hansen

Making the Most of Your "Now"

Knowing how short life is, it's important not to waste your "now." Don't waste it on pettiness, negativism, feelings of inferiority, fear of failure, regrets, or anything else that's destructive and doesn't really matter in the bigger picture of life. The less time you waste on things that get in the way of your goal, the more time you'll have to pursue it.

Don't listen to things that get in the way of your goal!

Before I knew the best part of my life had come,

it had gone.

◆

Ashleigh Brilliant

What a wonderful life I've had!

I only wish I'd realized it sooner.

◆

Colette

A life spent making mistakes is not only more honorable,

but more useful than a life spent doing nothing.

◆

George Bernard Shaw

Remember now your Creator

in the days of your youth.

—Ecclesiastes 12:1 NKJV

Time Marches On, but It Doesn't Have to Take Your Sense of Humor with It

Mature doesn't have to mean *boring*. In fact, the longer you live, the more material you're going to have to laugh about. So as you leave your school days behind, don't leave behind your sense of fun. Laughter is a requirement for life.

> If you carry your childhood with you, you never become older.
> **Abraham Sutzkever**

Laughter is a requirement for life.

91

THE where OF BEING A GRAD

Know where your goal is.
Know what it is you want to accomplish in life, and never forget it.

> **Unless you know where you are going,
> any road will take you there.**

Anonymous

Know Your Destination

Imagine a marathon in which the runners lined up at the starting point, the signal to begin was given, and everyone took off in different directions. The finish line was a mystery. No one knew where it was or how to get there. They just ran wherever they felt like running. No predetermined course, no signs, no maps—they just ran.

It would be a pretty confusing race, wouldn't it?

Imagine a football game with no goalposts or yardage markings. The players could run with the ball wherever they wanted to run with it. "Be free, running backs!" "Go with the wind, quarterbacks!" "Follow your destiny, O persons with shoulder pads!"

It would be a pretty ridiculous game, wouldn't it? No one would know in what direction to run or pass the ball, and it would be impossible to tell when a touchdown was scored.

Try playing baseball without bases, soccer or hockey without goals, or basketball without the basket. It just wouldn't make much sense, would it?

Just as we need direction and goals in sports, so we need them in life. We should know where we're headed. That doesn't mean that reaching the goal will be easy. Chances are it won't be. Who knows what kind of obstacles a football player will face on his way to the goal? The opposition could have some pretty large defensive players blocking his path. Still, he knows where the end zone is and keeps his sights set on it. A basketball player might encounter all sorts of obstacles while she tries to make her way to her basket, but she knows the basket is the goal. There's no question about that in her mind.

Know where your goal is. Don't lose sight of home plate, the finish line, or the end zone. Know what it is you want to accomplish in life, and never ever forget it.

There are no shortcuts
to any place worth going.

◆

Beverly Sills

Where to Go:
Decisions, Decisions, Decisions

Bible College: Institute of Higher Learning

Law School: THE BEST EDUCATORS BAR NONE

Police Academy: AN ARRESTING EXPERIENCE

Medical School: PRESCRIPTION FOR SUCCESS

Business School: WHERE YOU'LL BE KNOWN

BY THE COMPANY YOU KEEP

Veterinary School: A GREAT EDUCATION, BUT YOUR ROOMMATE COULD BE A PIG

No Language Barrier

For those who might be studying abroad, here are some phrases that might come in handy:

Petty cash fund unstable at this time.
Please send pizza money.

FRENCH: Le petite caisse subventionne instable en ce moment.
S'il vous plaît envoyer l'argent de pizza.

SPANISH: Caja chica financia inestable en este tiempo.
Mande por favor la pizza dinero.

GERMAN: Fundiert kleinliches Bargeld unsicher zur Zeit.
Schicken Sie bitte pizza Geld.

ITALIAN: La piccola cassa sovvenziona instabile a questo tempo.
Per favore di inviare il denaro di pizza.

Mailed laundry. Please return ASAP.

FRENCH: Mailed lessive.
S'il vous plaît le retour le plus tôt possible.

SPANISH: Envió ropa sucia.
Vuelva por favor tan pronto como sea posible.

GERMAN: Abgeschickte Wäscherei.
Kehren Sie bitte so bald wie möglich zurück.

ITALIAN: Il bucato di Mailed.
Per favore di ritornare al più presto possibile.

Grades? What grades?

FRENCH: Les degrés? Que gradue il?

SPANISH: ¿Los grados? ¿Qué gradúa?

GERMAN: Grade? Was stuft ein?

ITALIAN: I gradi? Che classifica?

Please disregard soon-to-be received letter from school president. Everyone recovered, and they're rebuilding the chemistry lab. All's well that ends well.
Love, Me

FRENCH: S'il vous plaît l'indifférence bientôt-à-est la lettre reçue du président d'école. Tout le monde a retrouvé et ils le reconstruire le laboratoire de chimie. Tout est bien qui finit bien.
L'amour, Je

SPANISH: Por favor indiferencia pronto a sea recibido carta del presidente de escuela. Todos recuperaron y ellos van a reedificar el laboratorio de la química. Todos están bien que terminan bien.
El amor, Mí

GERMAN: Beachtet bitte nicht angehenden empfangenen Brief von Schule
Präsidenten. Jeder hat und sie wiedererlangt'betr. Wiederaufbauen
vom Chemie Labor. Alle ist gut daß Enden gut.
Liebe, Mich

ITALIAN: Per favore la noncuranza presto-a-è ricevuto la lettera dal
presidente scolastico. Tutti ricuperato e loro'ricostruire di re il
laboratorio di chimica. Tutte il bene che le fini bene.
L'amore, Me

What Are You Waiting For?
Get Going!

Do what you can

with what you have

where you are.

◆

Theodore Roosevelt

Don't be afraid to take a big step if one is indicated; you can't cross a chasm in two small jumps.

David Lloyd George

Go Where No One Has Gone Before

Each generation has new inventions, new procedures, new products, and new ideas just waiting to be discovered. Don't be afraid to venture into these new territories. Go on, color outside the lines. Don't listen to those who are satisfied with the status quo or who say new ideas won't work. Dare to prove them wrong. Go beyond the knowledge of today and into the possibilities of tomorrow.

Do not follow where the path may lead.
Go, instead, where there is no path and leave a trail.

◆

Ralph Waldo Emerson

My alphabet starts with this letter called yuzz.
It's the letter I use to spell yuzz-a-ma-tuzz.
You'll be sort of surprised what there is to be found
Once you go beyond Z and start poking around.

◆

Dr. Seuss

Never tell a young person that something can't be done. God may have been waiting for centuries for somebody ignorant enough of the impossible to do that thing.

J. A. Holmes

You never test the resources of God

until you attempt the impossible.

F. B. Meyer

*Remember where you came from. In some ways
it's as important as knowing where you're headed.*

> **Remember your history.**
> **To forget is to not belong.**

Charlotte A. Black Elk

Remember Where You Came From

As you embark on this new adventure to regions unknown, it's important to remember where you came from. In some ways it's as important as knowing where you're headed.

Growing up, our parents or caregivers instilled in each of us certain values and a particular work ethic. They probably even influenced our attitudes to some extent. We may not agree with everything they did or believed, but those things on which we do agree shouldn't be left behind. Their influence on our lives is, in part, what made us who we are today.

So pack up all that encouragement, unconditional love, welcome and unwelcome advice, and all the prayers they gave you, and take them with you on your journey. They're your foundation. Don't try building a life without them.

Your faith will be a shock absorber for anything you might encounter along the way.

Wherever You Go, Take Your Faith Along

Whether you're continuing your education, starting your career, staying at home, or venturing off on a cross-country adventure, don't forget to take along your faith. It might not make the road smooth, but it will be a shock absorber for anything you might encounter along the way.

> *You will guide me with Your counsel, and afterward receive me to honor and glory.*
>
> —Psalm 73:24 Amp.

The LORD is your keeper;

The LORD is your shade at your right hand.

The sun shall not strike you by day,

Nor the moon by night.

The LORD shall preserve you from all evil;

He shall preserve your soul.

The LORD shall preserve your going out

and your coming in

From this time forth, and even forevermore.

—Psalm 121:5–8 NKJV

THE why OF BEING A GRAD

Apply your efforts in the direction of your dreams.

More men fail through lack of purpose than lack of talent.

Billy Sunday

Because Your Life Has a Purpose

It's hard to accomplish anything in life without a purpose. If you're not setting your sights on a specific target, chances are you're going to hit everything but that target. If your goal is to be an actor, chances are you'll have to take classes, go on auditions, and act in local productions while keeping down a steady job to pay the rent. If your goal is to be a doctor, real-estate training won't help you get a medical degree. You can't pass the bar exam by training in cosmetology or earn a beautician's license through a law school. Whatever your goal is, be sure you stay focused and apply your efforts in the direction of your dreams.

Striving for excellence motivates you; striving for perfection is demoralizing.

Harriet Braiker

Because You Can Do It

Don't you love the teachers who gave you a second chance? ("You didn't do very well on your test this week, so if you'd like to take it over and try to improve your score, I'll be giving it again next Wednesday.")

Of course you take him or her up on the offer. After all, this is your chance to change your grade—to do better. This time you'll study harder, get more rest the night before, and come to class better prepared. Why? Because you know you're being given a chance you don't really deserve. You don't want to mess up again.

Do you know that God gives us second chances too? Regardless of why we've messed up, the fact of the matter is, we have. But God offers us another chance. A chance to do better. A chance to change our ways. A chance to improve our attitudes. We don't deserve this second chance, but He still offers it to us. Why? Because second chances are what God and grace are all about.

Second chances are what God and grace are all about.

Life is my college. May I graduate well,
and earn some honors.

Louisa May Alcott

I have learned silence from the talkative, toleration from the intolerant, and kindness from the unkind.

Kahlil Gibran

Because Education Never Stops

Some of you may go to Harvard, while others may go to West Point. Some may choose to attend a culinary school, Bible college, state university, or community college. Or maybe you've already graduated from a school of higher learning. Some of you may have decided to go straight into your career or to marry and begin a family. You have freedom to go whichever direction you choose, but there's one university at which we've all passed the entrance exam and are right in the middle of our studies—the University of Life. Every day we're walking its campus, but we won't know our GPA until we get to the end of our schooling and graduate.

The University of Life—learn all you can, perform the best that you can, and do everything you can to leave it a better campus for those who follow.

I hope that my achievements in life shall be these—

that I will have fought for what was right and fair,

that I will have risked for that which mattered,

and that I will have given help to those

who were in need, that I will have left the earth

a better place for what I've done and

who I've been.

C. Hoppe

Be Teachable

If I could give you one word of advice for your life, it would be this—remain teachable.

If you're teachable, *even failure won't matter to you, because you'll know that you can learn something even from failure.*

If you're teachable, *you won't monopolize conversations but will be able to listen to others and learn from them. You already know what you know. Find out what others know.*

If you're teachable, *you'll respect the lessons that can be learned from the mistakes of others. You won't insist on having to experience them for yourself.*

If you're teachable, *specialists on every subject imaginable*

will cross your path at various times throughout your life. If you listen, they'll teach you their secrets—and it won't cost you a cent.

If you're teachable, you'll learn things about topics you didn't even know you were interested in.

If you're teachable, life will always be an adventure.

If you're teachable, you'll never stop growing.

If you're teachable, you will succeed every day because you have learned something new every day.

You can learn
new things at any time
in your life if you're willing
to be a beginner. If you actually
learn to like being a beginner,
the whole world
opens up to you.

Barbara Sher

There's a Lot to Learn

Elementary school graduate:
"I'VE GOT SO MUCH
MORE TO LEARN."

Junior high-school graduate:
"I KNOW EVERYTHING
THERE IS TO KNOW."

High-school graduate: "I HOPE I KNOW ENOUGH."

College graduate: "I'VE GOT SO MUCH MORE TO LEARN."

What we have done

for ourselves alone dies with us;

what we have done for others and the world

remains and is immortal.

Albert Pike

When it comes to giving,
some people stop at nothing.

Robert C. Savage

Because You Have So Much to Give

People who invest in the stock market are looking for a good return on their investment. Others may accumulate real estate, fine art, collectibles, or other valuable assets for the same reason. They want their investment to grow.

Do you realize that the people who have invested in you are looking for a good return on their investment too? They don't have stock riding on your performance, but they certainly have their hopes for a better world riding on it. They want their investment to grow and pay off in a life well lived and a generosity that's willing to pass years of learning on to future generations.

So take what you've been given and give something back to society. Invest in others. Keep the value of knowledge high.

Anyway

PEOPLE ARE ILLOGICAL,
UNREASONABLE, AND SELF-CENTERED.
Love them anyway.

IF YOU DO GOOD, PEOPLE WILL ACCUSE YOU
OF SELFISH ULTERIOR MOTIVES.
Do good anyway.

IF YOU ARE SUCCESSFUL,
YOU WILL WIN FALSE FRIENDS AND TRUE ENEMIES.
Succeed anyway.

THE GOOD YOU DO TODAY WILL BE FORGOTTEN TOMORROW.
Do good anyway.

HONESTY AND FRANKNESS MAKE YOU VULNERABLE.
Be honest and frank anyway.

THE BIGGEST MEN AND WOMEN WITH THE BIGGEST IDEAS CAN BE
SHOT DOWN BY THE SMALLEST MEN AND WOMEN WITH THE SMALLEST MINDS.
Think big anyway.

PEOPLE FAVOR UNDERDOGS BUT FOLLOW ONLY TOP DOGS.
Fight for a few underdogs anyway.

WHAT YOU SPEND YEARS BUILDING
MAY BE DESTROYED OVERNIGHT.
Build anyway.

PEOPLE REALLY NEED HELP BUT
MAY ATTACK YOU IF YOU DO HELP THEM.
Help people anyway.

GIVE THE WORLD THE BEST YOU HAVE
AND YOU'LL GET KICKED IN THE TEETH.
Give the world the best you have anyway.

–Kent M. Keith, from *Anyway: The Paradoxical Commandments*

**Someday, all that we will have is
what we have given to God.**

M. P. Horban

THE how OF BEING A GRAD

Ever feel like you're in over your head? So did Moses.

> **Some are born great, some achieve greatness,
> and some have greatness thrust upon them.**

William Shakespeare

How to Soar with Eagles
When You Feel like a Chicken Nugget

Ever feel like you're in over your head? You know God has a plan for your life. You even have a pretty good idea of what that plan might be. But you're convinced He's picked the wrong person for the task. What if you try and fail? What if you try again and fail again? And again? And again?

Remember Moses? God had a special purpose for Moses' life. The freedom of an entire nation was depending on his obedience to God's calling. But Moses felt unqualified. He was convinced God was depending on the wrong man for the job.

Do not fear,

for I am with you;

do not be dismayed,

for I am your God.

I will strengthen you

and help you;

I will uphold you with

my righteous right hand.

—Isaiah 41:10

"You want me to go and talk to Pharaoh? I can't do that. You saw the grades I got in public speaking in the palace school."

Moses didn't feel he was the right fit for God's plan. He had already settled for less than God's best, and he was fine with that. So why couldn't God just leave well enough alone?

God didn't want to leave Moses alone. He wanted bigger things for Moses than what Moses wanted for himself. God had faith in Moses. He knew the job He was giving him was Moses sized. It wasn't too big or too little. It was custom fitted just for him. In spite of Moses' feelings of inferiority, in spite of his past mistakes, God was determined to do everything He could to prevent Moses from settling for less than what he was capable of doing.

God doesn't want you to settle for less than what you're capable of accomplishing either. God has a purpose for your life, custom tailored for you. It's not a "one size fits all." It requires the exact qualities you have to offer, or ones you're capable of developing. It's a plan with your name on it—a plan that calls for you, not anyone else. You can either follow it or run from it. The choice is yours. If you decide to run, though, you should know this: Running doesn't change the fact that in God's eyes, you were capable—and that's one powerful endorsement.

Courage is being scared to death– and saddling up anyway.

John Wayne

News flash: God gave you gifts,
and He'll find a way to use them.

**Our part is the trusting;
it is God's part to accomplish the results.**

Hannah Whitall Smith

How to Verify the Flight Plan

What if you didn't "hear" God right? What if His plan for your life isn't what you think it is? What if you're supposed to be a staple stacker instead of playing in a band? Stacking staples may be steady employment, but if it's not what you had in mind, how do you pretend to be satisfied every day at work? Why would God give you musical talent and a desire to dedicate it to Him and then sit by and watch you waste it stacking staples hour after hour, day after day?

News flash: God doesn't give people gifts and then have no clue how He can put them to use.

If God gave you your gifts, and the Bible tells us He did, then He'll find a way to use them. Your job is to develop those talents to the best of your ability, be available, and trust His direction and timing. Whatever path He has chosen for you, it's the right path. It may not be the route you had mapped out, but if it's the one God has for you, it's the one you're supposed to take.

That's where trust comes in. You might not see how staple stacking is going to help you pursue your dream of becoming a musician, but trust that God might know something you don't. Maybe next month a customer will walk into that staple supply store, searching for the right kind of staples, and complain to you that he's having a lousy day—his drummer just quit the band. You'll talk drums for a few minutes. He'll ask if you play. You'll say yes. He'll laugh and say something like, "Hey, wanna take his place?" You'll laugh and say, "Are you serious?" And the next thing you know, you're in a band, right where you always wanted to be. Things like this happen all the time when you follow God's direction for your life.

So now, there you are, in a band. But it didn't come the way you thought it would. It came as a result of your obedience to God even in a staple-stacking career. You can see now why God wanted you to take that job in the first place. You didn't know why back then, but He did. And because this opportunity didn't come by the most direct route, there's no denying who gave you that job with the band. God did.

When it comes to our lives, we have limited vision. But God sees the big picture, and He knows the best path to get us to our final destination. It might not be the path we think He should use, or even the one most traveled; but it'll be the right one for us. We can trust Him with our dreams.

Keep praying,
but be thankful
that God's answers
are wiser than
your prayers.

William
Culbertson

How to Get Back in the Battle When You'd Rather Crawl Back into Bed

Writer Elinor Glyn, in a letter to the editor:

*Would you please publish the enclosed manuscript
or return it without delay, as I have other irons in the fire.*

Note from editor to Elinor:

Put this with your other irons.

Often the difference between those who succeed and those who fail isn't so much a matter of talent as it is a matter of perseverance. Many talented people will never achieve what they were meant to achieve because somewhere along the line, they allowed discouragement, rejection, or failure to turn their focus away from their goal. By the same token, hundreds of thousands of people with moderate gifts have succeeded not because of genius or talent but because they refused to give up.

They may have gotten knocked down, but they got right back up. They may have fumbled the ball, but they recovered it before it cost them the game. At some point in their lives, they determined that surrender wasn't an option, and in the end, they received the prize.

I have missed more than 9,000 shots in my career.
I have lost almost 300 games.
On 26 occasions I have been entrusted
to take the game's winning shot...and missed.
And I have failed over and over and over again in my life.
And that is why...
I succeed.

Michael Jordan

Those who trust in the LORD

are like Mount Zion,

which cannot be shaken

but endures forever.

—Psalm 125:1

Ten Surefire Ways to Fail in Life

1. Overlook your accomplishments.
2. Underestimate your potential.
3. Tell yourself you will fail.
4. Try to please everybody.
5. Undervalue your talents.
6. Scoff at your dreams.
7. Distrust your ideas.
8. Be afraid to try.
9. Sell out.
10. Quit.

Fall seven times, stand up eight.

Japanese proverb

Always leave something to wish for;
otherwise you will be miserable from your very happiness.

Baltasar Gracian

How Not to Hog the Road

Being the fastest runner in a marathon is certainly something to be proud of. Tripping the other runners so you can take the lead isn't. In other words, it's not just the fact that you achieve something in life; how you achieve it counts too. In fact, that counts most.

How you win counts too.
In fact, that counts most.

Be Fair

There are some men who, in a fifty-fifty proposition,

insist on getting the hyphen too.

◆

Lawrence J. Peter

Be Satisfied

The most pitiful poverty is that of a man who

has more than he needs but feels he doesn't have enough.

◆

Robert C. Savage

Be Generous

You can't live a perfect day without doing something

for someone who will never be able to repay you.

◆

John Wooden

> What is more mortifying than to feel that you have missed the plum for want of courage to shake the tree?

◆

Logan Pearsall Smith

How to Live with No Regrets

I once saw a commercial that featured a grandfather telling his grandchildren about all the adventurous things he did when he was young. The children were mesmerized. They hung on his every word until he finally confessed that those were just his dreams. He had never done any of them. He had

Dare to do things nobody else has done.

played it safe. It was obvious from the look on his face that in some ways, he regretted his caution.

You only get one chance at life. Don't be afraid to take risks. Be adventurous. Be safe when it comes to your health, of course, but dare to do things nobody has done. Explore new territory. Go where no one has gone before.

**If you just set out to be liked,
you would be prepared to compromise
on anything at any time,
and you would achieve nothing.**

Margaret Thatcher

How to Enjoy the Ride

How can you ensure that when you reach the end of your days, you'll be able to look back on a life filled with good memories, good friends, and few regrets? By making that your focus now.

Don't let a single moment slip through your fingers.

Don't want to regret not following your dream? Then follow it now.

Don't want to regret not keeping in touch with your friends? Then do everything you can to keep in touch now.

Don't want to regret not investing your money more wisely? Then invest it wisely now.

Don't want to look back on your life and realize you didn't enjoy it more? Then start enjoying it today.

You're writing your life story each day as you live it. It's not like a term paper that you don't get around to working on until the week before it's due. Life doesn't work that way. If you're going to enjoy the journey, you need to pay attention to it as it comes and not let a single moment slip through your fingers.

> There is no greater blunder than he who consumes
> the greater part of his life getting his living.
>
> ◆
>
> **Henry David Thoreau**

> Leisure, some degree of it,
> is necessary to the health of every man's spirit.
>
> ◆
>
> **Harriet Martineau**

> Unless each day can be looked back upon by an individual
> as one in which he has had some fun,
> some joy, some real satisfaction,
> that day is a loss.
>
> ◆
>
> **Dwight D. Eisenhower**

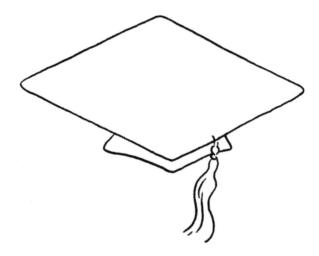

Every day I live I am more convinced
that the waste of life lies in the love we have not given,
the powers we have not used,
the selfish prudence that will risk nothing and which,
shirking pain, misses happiness as well.

Mary Cholmondeley

The Last Word on Being a Grad

Advance Token to Go

Your schooling, or at least this part of it, is behind you now. Before you lies a world of possibilities. Some of them have your name on them. Go after them. Live the life you were destined to live. It won't be perfect. I've often said that life is like an electrocardiogram. It has its ups and it has its downs. If it ever stays level for too long, you're probably no longer with us. So go on, walk into your future. Your life awaits you.

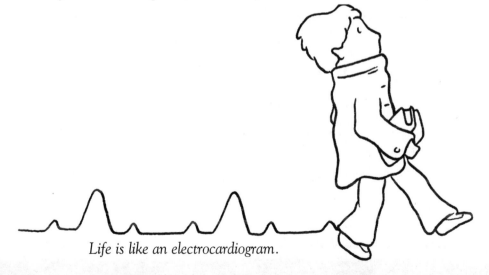

Life is like an electrocardiogram.

◆ Free Self-Serve Laundry Services ◆

Bearer is entitled to use laundry facilities free of charge,
*provided clothing is not left in the machines for more than
one twenty-four-hour period. Lint trap should be cleaned after each use,
and no red item shall be washed with white towels.
Failure to comply with the above stipulations
may result in immediate termination of privileges.*

◆ All-Access Refrigerator Pass ◆

**Bearer of this pass shall be given access
to all areas of the refrigerator,**
*provided ample consideration is given to other parties in the household.
Should it be determined that the shelves require replenishment too often,
owners of refrigerator shall have the right to padlock
the appliance and revoke the pass.*

◆ Free Meal Pass ◆

**Bearer of this pass is entitled to come home
and eat with the family**

*on any date, for any meal. No reservations needed.
No complaining allowed.*

◆ Free Advice ◆

Bearer of this coupon is entitled to free parental-type advice.

*Available twenty-four hours.
No age limit. Unlimited use. Unused advice is non-returnable.*

◆ Free Pet-Sitting Service ◆

Bearer is entitled to free pet-sitting service,

*provided the pet or pets have already been established
as part of the family. Newly acquired boa constrictors not included.*

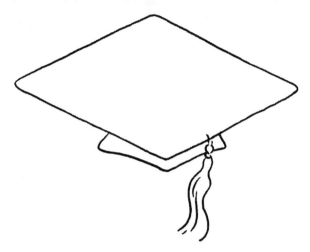

Invitation

The honor of your presence is requested…

When: NOW

Duration: FIRST BREATH TO LAST

Location: YOUR BODY, MIND, AND SPIRIT

For: YOUR LIFE

No substitutions allowed.
It's your life! Don't miss it!

Generic Valedictorian Speech

We, the class of _____*(fill in year) are gathered here today to…*

- ❑ celebrate the achievements of many.
- ❑ honor our fellow students and educators.
- ❑ see how many video cameras we can have operating in a single place at a single time.

We've learned a lot over these past…

- ❑ two years.
- ❑ three years.
- ❑ four years.
- ❑ Does it really matter how long it took us?

We realize we are leaving behind so many…

- ❑ beloved teachers.
- ❑ lifelong friends.
- ❑ tuna sandwiches in our lockers.

And although we are going to miss all the…

- ❑ late-night studying,
- ❑ pop quizzes,
- ❑ classroom naps,

we know we will return someday to…
- ❑ get in touch with our roots.
- ❑ reconnect with friends and family.
- ❑ do our laundry.

When we do, we know you'll see that we have…
- ❑ grown and matured.
- ❑ achieved our goals.
- ❑ spent all our money and need a loan.

But until then, we still have our…
- ❑ fond memories.
- ❑ dreams.
- ❑ overdue library books.

We thank you for joining us in our…
- ❑ celebration.
- ❑ graduation festivities.
- ❑ faculty polka.

You'll never know what your…
- ❑ presence here today
- ❑ encouragement
- ❑ monetary gift of more than $50
  …has meant to us.

Now it's time for us to venture off into…

❑ a world filled with possibilities.

❑ a life filled with adventure.

❑ a parking lot filled with gridlocked traffic.

But before we go, we'd like to share this final thought:

❑ Thank you for all you've done to make this moment possible.

❑ Farewell, but not good-bye.

❑ We don't really have to get a job tomorrow, do we?

The Last Word on Being a Grad

Bill of Rights for Parents of Graduates

The parents of the graduate shall have the right to whistle and wave from the balcony in a manner that will draw the student's attention. Swinging from the balcony and yelling, "That's my kid!" during the ceremony is, for obvious safety reasons, discouraged.

Parents of the graduate shall have the right to mail announcements, distribute flyers, appear on television talk shows, and rent billboards heralding the happy occasion.

During the ceremony, parents of the graduate shall have the right to stand at the calling out of their child's name and to begin singing the "Hallelujah Chorus." They should, however, make every attempt to stay on key.

Parents of the graduate shall have the unalienable right to brag about their child's achievement whenever they can work it into a conversation. Please note, however, that telling it to information operators will only tie up the line for the rest of the population.

Parents of the graduate shall have the right to place bumper stickers on their car announcing that they are the proud parents of a graduate. When doing this, it's a good idea to make sure *graduate* is spelled correctly.

Parents of the graduate shall have the right to call every relative in their family tree, excluding deceased relations. They rarely send gifts anyway.

Parents of the graduate shall have the right to cheer as loudly as they want, party as long as they choose, and cry as often as they need to. It's their right. They've earned it!

Suggested Graduation Gifts

The Gift of Laughter

*If I were given the opportunity to present a gift to the next generation,
it would be the ability for each individual to learn to laugh at himself.*

◆

Charles Schulz

The Gift of Friendship

A friend is a second self.

◆

Aristotle

The Gift of Perseverance

*There are two ways of meeting difficulties:
you alter the difficulties, or you alter yourself to meet them.*

◆

Phyllis Bottome

The Gift of Wonder

*You cannot help but learn more as you take the world into your hands.
Take it up reverently, for it is an old piece of clay,
with millions of thumbprints on it.*

◆

John Updike

The Gift of Ambition

The dictionary is the only place that success comes before work.
Hard work is the price we must pay for success.
I think you can accomplish anything if you're willing to pay the price.

◆

Vince Lombardi

The Gift of Faith

God cannot give us happiness
and peace apart from Himself,
because it is not there.

◆

C. S. Lewis

The Gift of Courage

Courage is fear that has said its prayers.

◆

Ruth Fishel

The Gift of Today

Each day comes bearing its own gifts.
Untie the ribbons.

◆

Ruth Ann Schabacker

You're on your way!